BEAR'S NEW HOME

BOOK ONE OF BEAR'S JOURNEY

BY KRYSTLE SCROGGINS
ILLUSTRATED BY CHARU JAIN

Since I have become a part of the family, I have learned about Jesus and the Word of God. My parents read it daily and talk about Him all of the time. So when I look back at events throughout my life, I can now see how His Word is evident in my life story. I hope you can enjoy these books and see how He works in your life, too! 1 John 5:13, "I write these things to you who believe in the Name of the Son of God so that you may know that you have eternal life."

Love, Bear

Ah, yes, I remember the day my life truly began. It all started when I was a young pup of about seven weeks old. I spent my days with my brothers and sisters playing and napping. Then one morning my world changed.

The owner picked me up and put me in the bathtub. He squirted some of that smell-good stuff on my fur and it got all bubbly while he scrubbed.
What's all this about?

Before I knew it, I was getting rinsed off. I gave a big shake to get the water off of me and I saw water go everywhere! After rubbing me all over with the towel, the man put a blue bow around my neck.

We stepped out onto the big front porch. Their house was situated on the side of a Tennessee hill and we could see God's country for miles.

I noticed two people making their way up the driveway and across the deck. The lady's eyes filled with tears as she took me into her arms and I instantly snuggled against her. We followed the man inside where he showed them my parents and all my siblings.

We loaded up in the car and I found myself being whisked away. I heard the grand tale of how I had been chosen out of the many puppies we left behind. These two humans, who I now call my mom and dad, searched for weeks for the right puppy.

My mom said that my dad showed her a picture of the puppy he liked and it was the very same picture she was planning to show him. It was me!

How great it is to be handpicked for a family; God did this for you, too!! And He (our Heavenly Father) chose us to be His very own, joining us to Himself even before He laid the foundation of the universe! Ephesians 1:4 (TPT)

The drive was a long one with many stops for me to have a break. During the drive, I could hear them discuss naming me. After looking me over a bit, they gave me the name Bear.

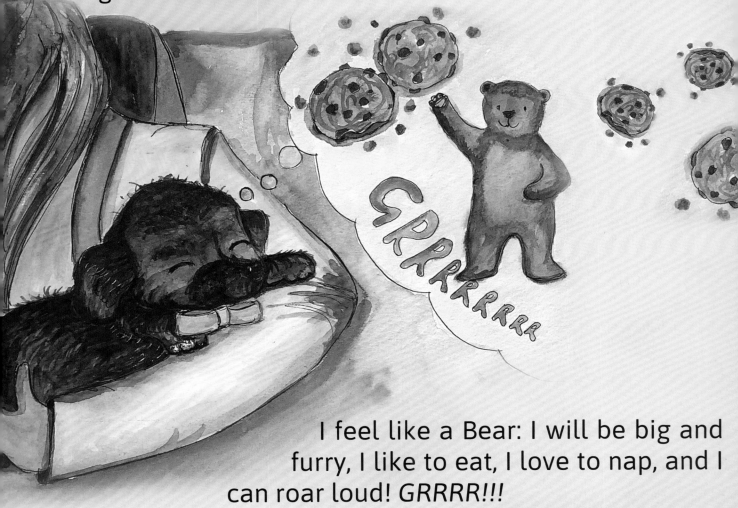

I feel like a Bear: I will be big and furry, I like to eat, I love to nap, and I can roar loud! *GRRRR!!!*

Finally, after the eight-hour car ride, we arrived at my new home. My mom scooped me up to carry me inside where we were met at the door by a strange woman. A gray-headed lady took me from my mom and held me tight. I noticed her face light up when she kept talking about how cute I was.

Why yes, yes I am, thank you!

I heard noises coming from across the room. A door slid open and two boys came running towards me. The smaller boy kept trying to pick me up and squeezed a little too tight. *Who are all these people and why do they keep petting and hugging me?*

I quickly learned the boys were my new brothers and the lady is called Granny. I felt like the star of the show, their new prize and I loved their attention!

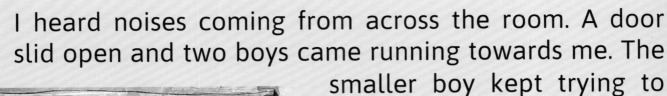

God, our Heavenly Father, should be even greater than this feeling in our lives. He should always be the center of our focus and affection. Revelation 4:11 says, "You are worthy, our Lord and God, to receive glory, honor, and power, for You created all things, and by Your plan they were created and exist."

After my new brothers played with me a bit, they let me outside one more time and then we called it a night.

2 Peter 3:13, "But according to His promise we are waiting for new heavens and a new earth in which righteousness dwells."

I have a goal to make the most of my time with my family and grow in my faith. God's Word says in Matthew 11:29, "Simply join your life with mine. Learn my ways and you'll discover that I'm gentle, humble, easy to please. You will find refreshment and rest in Me."

Bear is a St Berdoodle, which is a St Bernard and Poodle mix. He loves milkbones and any table-scraps. His past times include chewing on buffalo horns, playing with his brothers, napping, and getting into his mom's personal space at all times.

Krystle

First time author, Krystle is a daughter of the King, wife, and mother of two boys. She loves to spend time with her family, read, write, gardening, different crafts, travel and she loves animals. Krystle and her family are a part of Kingdom Encounter Ministries based out of Rockwall, TX.

Charu Jain

Charu Jain is a passionate and self taught watercolor illustrator from India.She loved creating this beautiful book on Bear ,she has a whimsical style which you can see in her work. She has an instantly recognisable style with fun and colourful characters. Her inspiration is Beatrix Potter, E. H . Shepard , Quentin Blake and Roald Dahl.